Wonders

Cover and Title Page: Nathan Love

www.mheonline.com/readingwonders

McGraw Hill Education

Send all inquiries to:
McGraw-Hill Education
2 Penn Plaza
New York, NY 10121

ISBN: 978-0-02-130729-6
MHID: 0-02-130729-6

Printed in the United States of America.

7 8 9 10 LKV 26 25   D

Wonders

ELD
Companion Worktext

Program Authors

Diane August

Jana Echevarria

Josefina V. Tinajero

McGraw Hill Education

Unit 5

What's Next?

(t) age fotostock/SuperStock; (c) NASA-GFSC Image created by Reto Stockli with the help of Alan Nelson, under the leadership of Fritz Hasler; (b) Kirk Weddle/Photodisc/Getty Images

1

What's Next?

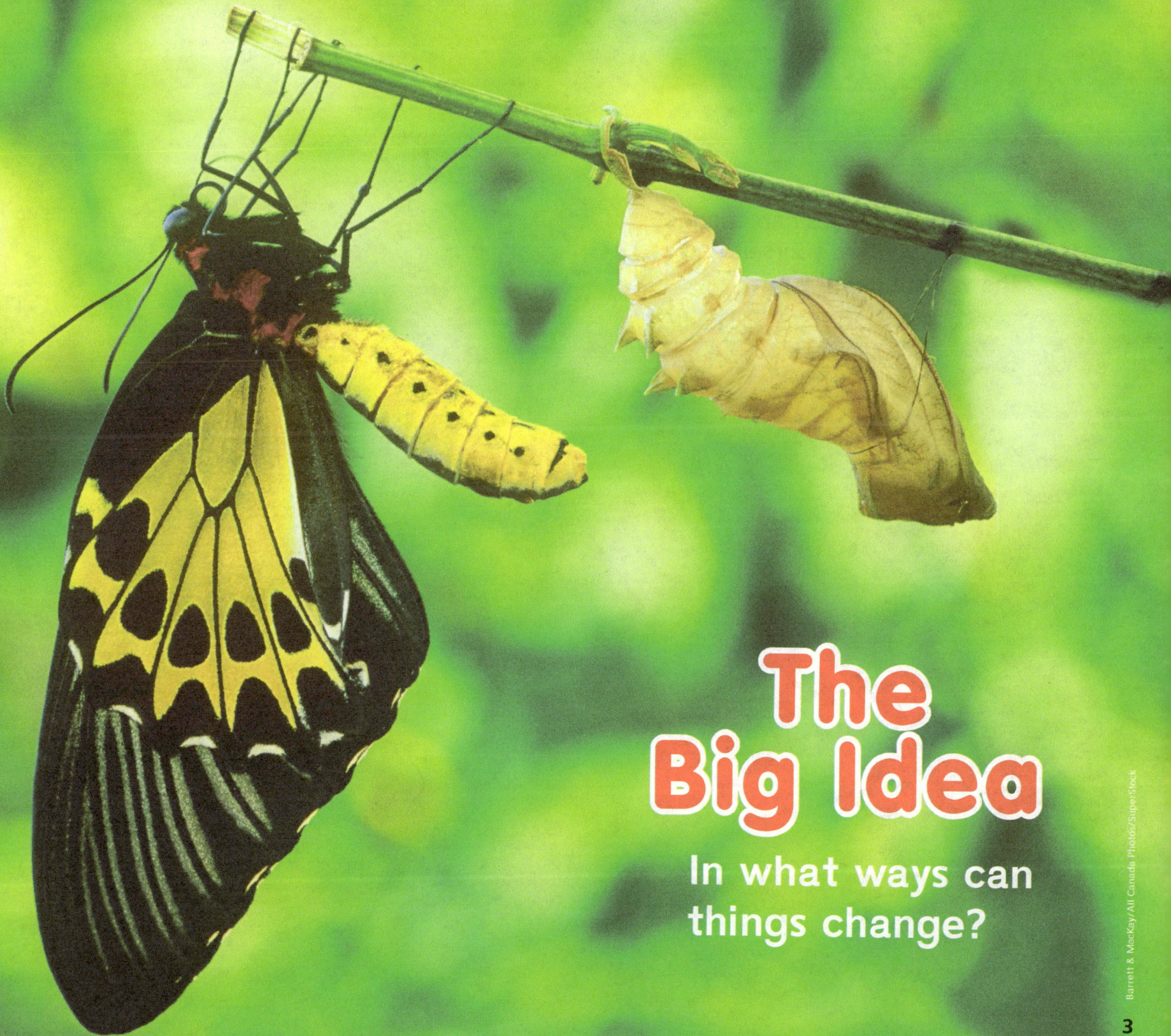

The Big Idea

In what ways can things change?

Weekly Concept New Perspectives

? Essential Question

What experiences can change the way you see yourself and the world around you?

>> *Go Digital*

4

What can the people see from the top of a building that they can't see from the ground? Write in the chart what happens when you see things from a new view, or perspective.

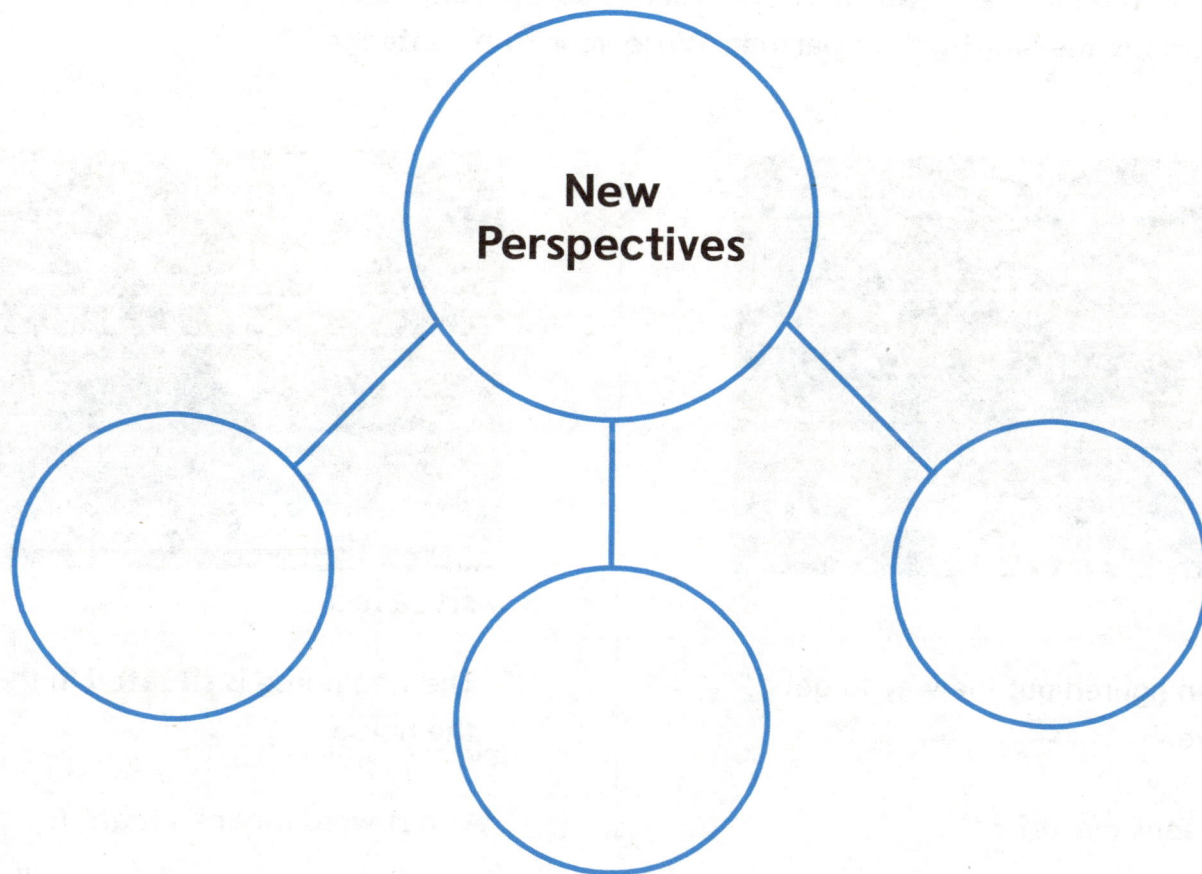

New Perspectives

Discuss how a new view, or perspective, helps you to see the world differently. Use words from the chart. You can say:

From the top of a building, people can see _____.

From the ground people can see _____.

A new perspective helps people see _____.

More Vocabulary

COLLABORATE

Look at the picture. Read the word. Then read the sentence. Talk about the word with a partner. Write your own sentence.

clever

The **clever** man figured out the way to get out of the maze.

What word means *clever*?

foolish   smart   quick

What does a clever person do?

A clever person solves a _____

_____.

situated

The tree house is **situated** in the backyard of the house.

What word means *situated*?

located   marked   collected

Where is the school playground situated?

The school playground is *situated* _____

_____.

Words and Phrases: *until* and *used to*

The word *until* means "up to the time of."

How long did the students stay in the classroom?

They stayed in the classroom **until** the school bell rang.

The phrase *used to* means "something that happened in the past does not happen now."

Is Grandpa writing a letter?

No, Grandpa **used to** write letters. Now he sends emails.

COLLABORATE Look at the picture. Then read the sentence. Talk with a partner. Write the word that completes each sentence.

Kevin grew an inch this year. He _____ _____ be shorter.

until   used to

Rosa sleeps _____ her alarm clock buzzes.

until   used to

COLLABORATE

1 Talk About It

Look at the picture. Read the title. Talk about what you see. Use these words.

friends   middle school

students

Write about what you see.

I see _____

_____

_____.

When do students go to middle school?

Students go to middle school when

_____

_____.

Take notes as you read the story.

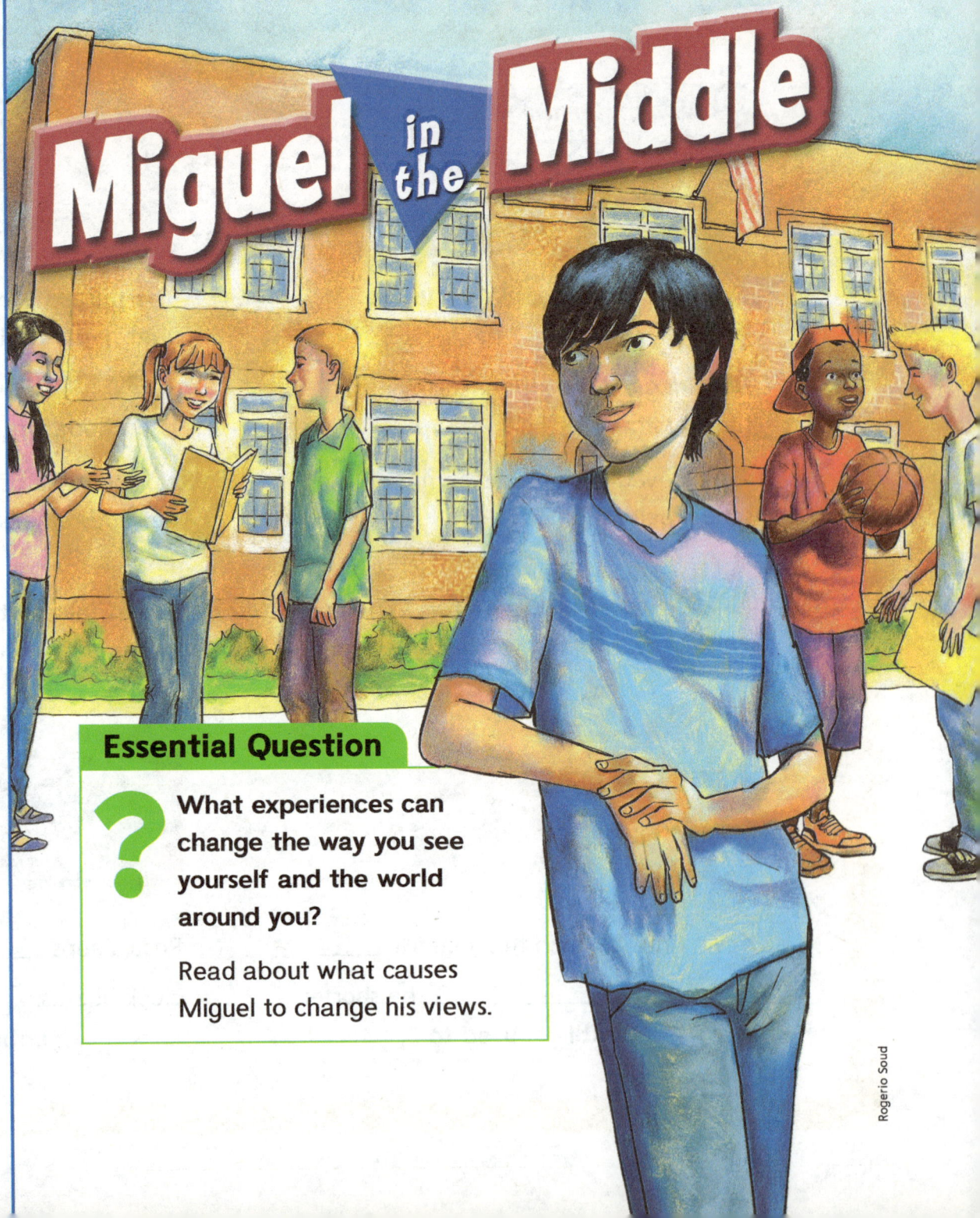

Miguel in the Middle

Essential Question

? What experiences can change the way you see yourself and the world around you?

Read about what causes Miguel to change his views.

Rogerio Soud

I'm always in the middle. I'm the middle child in my family. I always sit in the middle of my classroom. My first and last names, Miguel Martinez, start with M. And, the letter M is the middle letter of the alphabet.

I'm also in the middle of a large circle of friends. Most of them were my classmates until this year. You see, we started middle school in September. My closest friends go to a different middle school in the area, because of the way our school district is mapped out. Now the only classmate I know is Jake. He's a genius in math, but math is not my favorite subject. So we never became friends.

Another change is that I'm also no longer **situated** in the middle of the classroom. My seat is in the front row. Also, the new teachers give us a lot more homework than we used to get, especially math homework.

Text Evidence

1 Sentence Structure A C T

Reread the first two sentences in the second paragraph. Who does *them* refer to? Circle the text in the first sentence. What do you learn about them in the second sentence? Underline the text.

The pronoun them refers to _____

_____, and they

were _____.

2 Specific Vocabulary A C T

The phrase *You see* tells that the speaker will give an explanation. Circle the explanation Miguel gives.

Miguel explains why _____

_____.

3 Comprehension
Compare and Contrast

Reread the last paragraph. Underline the sentences that tell how the new school is different from the old school.

9

1 Sentence Structure A C T

Reread the second and third paragraphs. Jake finishes Miguel's question. Circle the text. What did Miguel want to ask Jake?

Miguel wanted to ask _____

_____ .

2 Specific Vocabulary A C T

The word *session* means "a period of time spent on an activity." What happened during the study session? Underline the text that tells you. What did Miguel learn?

After the study session, Miguel

_____ .

3 Comprehension

Reread the fifth paragraph. Why was the teacher surprised when Miguel raised his hand?

She was surprised because _____

_____

_____ .

By the end of October, Jake and I were good friends. It happened because I am hopeless at math, especially fractions. So one day, I approached Jake after school.

I began, "Hey, Jake, I was wondering if you could—"

"Help you with the math homework?" he said, completing my sentence. "I'd be happy to help you, Miguel."

I was surprised because I wasn't sure that Jake even knew my name. That night, Jake and I had a study session. Jake's a superb math teacher. He used slices of a pizza to explain fractions. By the end of the night, I fully understood why eight-sixteenths is the same as one-half!

The next day in class, our teacher put math problems on the board, and I solved one problem. She was surprised when I raised my hand with the answer. So was I!

Rogerio Soud

I can't believe winter vacation is almost here! Lately, school has been fun, especially math. I used to look forward to a school break. Now, I feel sad that I'll be away from school.

The other day, the most amazing thing happened when our teacher gave us a math brainteaser. She asked, "If you wrote all the numbers from one to one hundred, how many times would you write number nine?"

Most students said ten, although some clever kids said eleven, because they realized that ninety-nine has two nines. Only Jake and I had the correct answer—twenty! Everyone else forgot to count all the nineties.

Jake and I plan to hang out together during winter break. He promised to show me the Math Museum. All my new friends from middle school will come, too. You see, although I have a completely different perspective on math, some things haven't changed. I'm still in the middle of a large circle of friends!

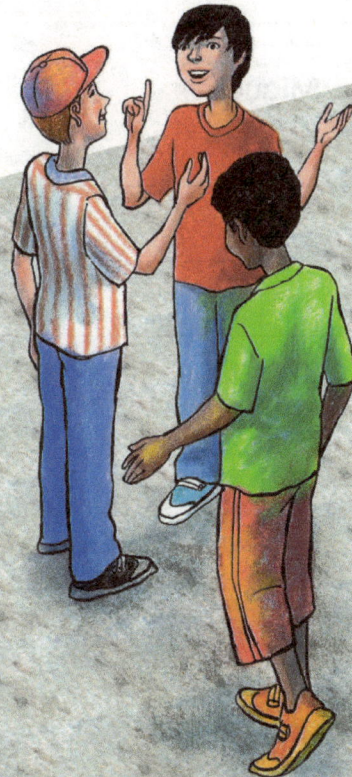

Make Connections

? Discuss how Miguel changed after entering middle school. What caused him to change? **ESSENTIAL QUESTION**

When has a new place changed the way you see yourself? **TEXT TO SELF**

Text Evidence

1 Specific Vocabulary A C T

The phrase *look forward to* means "to be excited about something that will happen." What did Miguel look forward to? Circle the text. How has his feeling changed?

Miguel used to look forward to

_____,

but now _____.

2 Sentence Structure A C T

Reread the first sentence in the third paragraph. Why did some kids answer eleven? Underline the text. Why are they wrong?

They are wrong because _____

_____.

COLLABORATE

3 Talk About It

Reread the last paragraph. Discuss how Jake and Miguel's friendship changed.

Respond to the Text

Partner Discussion Work with a partner. Read the questions about "Miguel in the Middle." Show where you found text evidence. Write the page numbers. Then discuss what you read.

At the beginning of the story, how did Miguel feel?

At the new school Miguel didn't have any _____.

Miguel did not like math because _____.

Miguel was not friends with Jake because _____.

Text Evidence 🔍

Page(s): _____

Page(s): _____

Page(s): _____

How did Jake help to change Miguel?

Jake taught Miguel by _____.

Miguel liked to do math because _____

_____.

Text Evidence 🔍

Page(s): _____

Page(s): _____

Group Discussion Present your answers to the group. Cite text evidence for your ideas. Listen to and discuss the group's opinions.

Write Work with a partner. Look at your notes about "Miguel in the Middle." Write your answer to the Essential Question. Use text evidence to support your answer. Use vocabulary words in your writing.

What experiences changed how Miguel felt about middle school?

Miguel was not happy at the new school because _____

_____.

Jake helped Miguel with _____.

Miguel learned to like math because _____.

In the end, Miguel liked going to school because _____

_____.

Share Writing Present your writing to the class. Discuss their opinions. Talk about their ideas. Explain why you agree or disagree with their ideas. You can say:

I agree with _____.

I do not agree because _____.

Write to Sources

Gilbert

Take Notes About the Text I took notes about the text on the chart to answer the question: *Do you think Miguel was happy to go to middle school?*

pages 8–11

Text Clue	Opinion
Miguel's friends go to a different middle school.	Miguel does not have friends. He is lonely.
Teachers give students a lot more homework.	Miguel is not happy about having a lot of homework.
Miguel and Jake become friends. Miguel likes math. Miguel feels sad about the school break.	Miguel likes middle school because things are better at school.

Write About the Text I used notes from my chart to write an opinion about Miguel.

Student Model: *Opinion*

At the beginning, Miguel was not happy to attend middle school. Now, he is happy because things are better. Miguel's friends were his classmates in elementary school, but in middle school he did not have any friends. Also, he got a lot more homework. I think he felt lonely.

Then I think things got better and his feelings changed. I know because he and Jake became friends. Miguel learned to like math. He was sad about the school break.

TALK ABOUT IT

Text Evidence

Draw a box around a sentence that comes from the notes. Does this clue support Gilbert's opinion?

Grammar

Circle words that tell sequence in the first two sentences. Do verbs in the sentences match sequence?

Condense Ideas

Underline the two sentences that tell Gilbert's opinion. How can you condense the ideas into one sentence?

Your Turn

Do you think Miguel will continue to do well in school? Write your opinion. Use text evidence in your writing.

>> Go Digital
Write your response online. Use your editing checklist.

? **Essential Question**
How do shared experiences help people adapt to change?

>> *Go Digital*

What are the people in the photograph doing? Is it good to share an experience with other people? How can sharing experiences help you adapt to change? Write your answers in the chart.

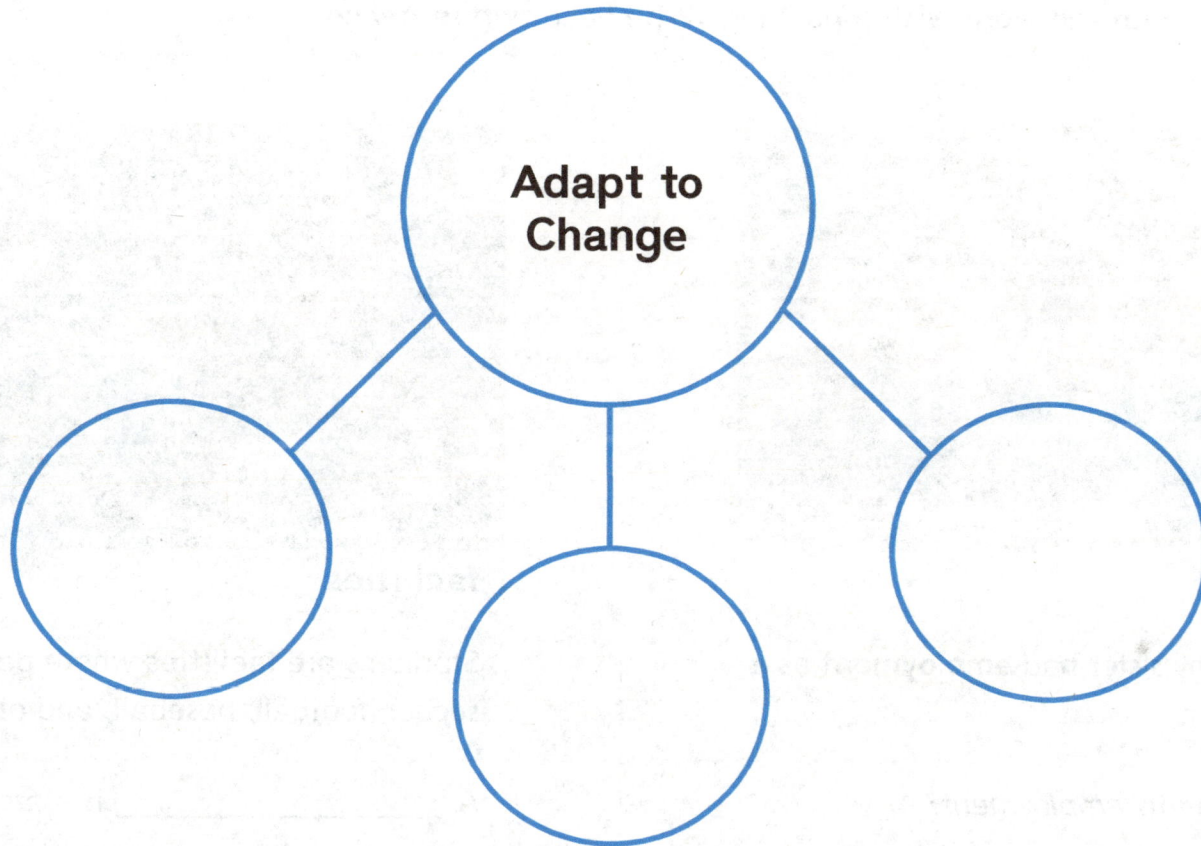

Adapt to Change

Discuss how sharing experiences helps people adapt to change. Use words from the chart. Complete the sentences.

When people share experiences, they can support _____.

Then, people can adapt to change because they don't feel _____

_____.

COLLABORATE Look at the picture. Read the word. Then read the sentence.
Talk about the word with a partner. Write your own sentence.

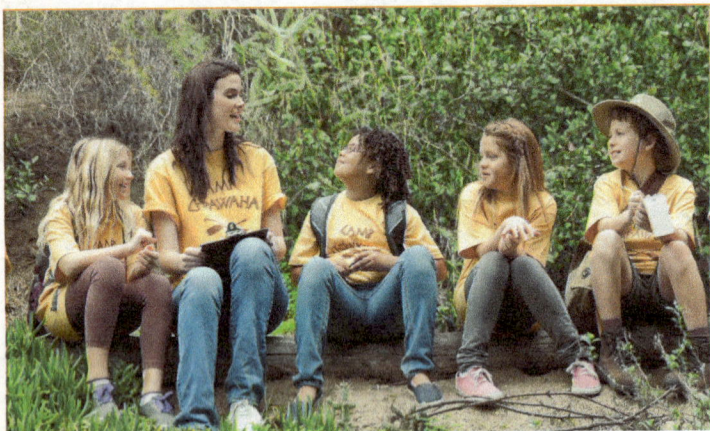

employment

Last summer my sister had **employment** as a camp counselor.

What word means *employment*?

paper   job   information

What kind of employment do you want to have during summer?

During summer I want to work as a _____

_____ for employment.

facilities

Stadiums are **facilities** where people play soccer, football, baseball, and other sports.

A _____ is a *facility* in a park.

soccer field   tree   dog

What facilities are in your school?

_____ are facilities in our school.

Words and Phrases: *go along* and *hard times*

The phrase *go along* means "to go or travel with someone."

What does the dog want?

The dog wants to **go along** to the lake.

Hard times means "a time when people have difficulties or troubles"

What caused hard times during the Great Depression?

One cause of **hard times** was unemployment.

COLLABORATE **Look at the picture. Read the sentence. Talk with a partner. Write the word that completes the sentence.**

Zack wants to _____ with his sister to the beach.

go along   hard times

It is helpful to talk to friends during _____.

go along   hard times

Kei Uesugi/Photodisc/Getty Images; American Stock/Archive Photos/Getty Images; Laurence Mouton/Getty Images; Tom Merton/OJO Images/Getty Images

The Day the Rollets Got Their Moxie Back

1 Talk About It

Look at the picture. Read the title. Discuss what you see. Use these words.

family   girls   letter   communicate

Write about what you see.

This story is about _____

_____.

What are the girls doing?

They are _____

_____.

How do you communicate with family members who are far away?

I communicate by _____

_____.

Take notes as you read the story.

Essential Question

? **How do shared experiences help people adapt to change?**

Read about how members of a family support each other during hard times.

Ron Mazellan

20

Sometimes, the thing that helps you through hard times comes like a bolt from the blue. My older brother's letter was like that. It was 1937, and Ricky was in Wyoming building **facilities** for a new state park. This project was part of President Roosevelt's **employment** program that created jobs for young men like Ricky. Unfortunately, it didn't help our dad find work.

I imagined Ricky turning trees into lumber, with mountains, blue sky, and evergreen trees all around him. It almost made me want to become a lumberjack.

While my older sister Ruth and I read Ricky's letter, Dad sat silently in his chair. "Shirley, Ricky was in a talent show, and he wore a grass skirt and did a hula dance while playing the ukulele!" Ruth exclaimed with delight. "I bet he was the cat's pajamas!"

"Let's have our own talent show!" I replied.

Mom called from the kitchen, "I'll sew some grass skirts. Now come set the table for dinner."

1 Sentence Structure (A C T)

Reread the last sentence in the first paragraph. What does *it* refer to? Circle the text. Why didn't *it* help Dad? Underline the text.

It didn't help Dad because _____

_____.

2 Specific Vocabulary (A C T)

A *lumberjack* is a person who cuts trees to make wood and lumber. Underline the context clues that help you figure out the meaning.

A lumberjack works _____

_____.

3 Comprehension

Compare and Contrast

Reread the third paragraph. Put a box around the text that tells what Dad and the girls are doing. How are their moods different?

Dad feels _____, while

the girls feel _____.

① Sentence Structure Ⓐ Ⓒ Ⓣ

Reread the second sentence. Mom speaks informally and leaves out some words. Rewrite the question by adding the missing words.

_____

_____

② Specific Vocabulary Ⓐ Ⓒ Ⓣ

The word *meatless* has the suffix *-less,* which means "without." Why did Mom call the dinner a "meatless meat loaf"? Underline the text that tells you.

Mom made the loaf with _____

_____.

③ Comprehension

Compare and Contrast

Reread the last paragraph. Circle Dad's and the girls' reasons for going to the soup kitchen. Compare the reasons.

_____

_____

Dad stayed in his chair. Mom asked with sympathy, "Any jobs in the paper?" Dad shook his head no. He had worked in the theater as an artist, but jobs like his were now gone.

Mom served a baked loaf of beets. "It's beet loaf, the meatless meat loaf," she said as she served up slices.

Ruth fidgeted in her seat, excited about the talent show. Though I was calm on the outside, inside I was excited, too.

Over the next week, Ruth and I practiced our Hawaiian dance. On Saturday, Dad decided to grin and bear it, and grab some hot coffee at the local soup kitchen. He hoped to hear about available jobs there. Ruth and I begged to go along because the kitchen served doughnuts and hot chocolate on weekends, and Dad agreed.

Ron Mazellan

Everyone in line was dressed for the cold weather. Many people wore two or three layers of clothing. Dad and the other men bowed their heads as if in shame.

The line moved slowly. Ruth was bored and she began practicing her dance steps, so I sang an upbeat tune to give her some music. Around us, people began to smile. Soon, folks clapped along. Ruth felt encouraged by the crowd, so she twirled and swayed like there was no tomorrow.

"Those girls sure have moxie!" someone shouted.

"They've got heart, all right!" offered another.

"Those are my girls!" Dad declared proudly.

Everyone applauded. For those short moments, the past didn't matter, and the future looked bright. I couldn't wait to write to Ricky and tell him the news.

Make Connections

? Talk about how Ricky, Ruth, and Shirley adapted to the situation. **ESSENTIAL QUESTION**

Think about when people helped you adapt to a new situation. Compare your experience with the Rollet family's. **TEXT TO SELF**

1 Comprehension
Compare and Contrast

Reread the last sentence of the first paragraph. How are Dad and the other men alike? Underline the text that tells you.

Dad and the other men _____

_____.

2 Specific Vocabulary **A C T**

The word *moxie* means "spirit or energy." How did the girls show they have moxie? Underline text in the second paragraph that shows the girls have moxie.

COLLABORATE

3 Talk About It

Discuss how the girls' song and dance helped Dad and the folks in line. Then write about it.

Dad and the folks in line _____

_____

_____.

Respond to the Text

Partner Discussion Work with a partner. Read the questions about "The Day the Rollets Got Their Moxie Back." Show where you found text evidence. Write the page numbers. Then discuss what you read.

COLLABORATE

What news did Ricky share? How did his news affect his family?

Text Evidence 🔍

Ricky wrote about _____.

Page(s): _____

Shirley and Ruth decided to _____.

Page(s): _____

Their mother offered _____.

Page(s): _____

What happened while the family waited in line for the soup kitchen?

Text Evidence 🔍

Shirley _____ and Ruth _____

Page(s): _____

for the people, while they _____.

Dad and the others felt _____.

Page(s): _____

COLLABORATE **Group Discussion** Present your answers to the group. Cite text evidence for your ideas. Listen to and discuss the group's opinions.

Write Work with a partner. Look at your notes about "The Day the Rollets Got Their Moxie Back." Write your answer to the Essential Question. Use text evidence to support your answer. Use vocabulary words in your writing.

How did the Rollet family help each other adapt to changes during hard times?

Ricky's letter inspired Shirley and Ruth to _____

_____.

At the line for the soup kitchen, Shirley and Ruth _____

_____.

Shirely and Ruth helped Dad and the others feel _____.

Dad was proud because the girls _____

_____.

Share Writing Present your writing to the class. Discuss their opinions. Talk about their ideas. Explain why you agree or disagree with their ideas. You can say:

I agree with _____.

I do not agree because _____.

Write to Sources

Bree

pages 20–23

Take Notes About the Text I took notes about the text on the chart to respond to the prompt: *Write a new scene during dinner. Include a dialogue between Ruth and Shirley.*

Text Clues	New Scene
Ricky wrote about a talent show. He wore a grass skirt, danced, and played a ukulele. Shirley and Ruth want to have a talent show.	Ruth wants to dance for the talent show with Shirley. Shirley wants to find a song. Ruth wants to start now.
Dad was worried because there were no jobs in the newspaper.	Dad was quiet during dinner. He looked worried.
Mom made a beet loaf.	Mom tells Ruth and Shirley to finish dinner.

Write About the Text I used notes from my chart to write a a new scene during dinner.

Student Model: *Narrative Text*

As we ate dinner, Ruth said, "I can't wait to put on a talent show. I can dance. Shirley, do you want to dance with me?"

I said, "Before you start dancing, you need some music. Why don't we look for a song?"

Ruth jumped up from the table. She said, "OK. Let's get started."

Mom told Ruth and me, "You need to finish your dinner first. Sit down and eat, please." Dad ate silently. He was worried.

TALK ABOUT IT

COLLABORATE

Text Evidence
Draw a box around a sentence that comes from the notes. Did Bree use the information to write a new scene?

Grammar
Circle the pronoun *I*. Who does the pronoun refer to? Is this person the narrator?

Connect Ideas
Underline Ruth's first dialogue. How can you combine the sentences and connect the ideas?

Your Turn

COLLABORATE

Add a scene to the end of the story. Write about what Dad tells Mom about Shirley and Ruth at the soup kitchen. Use details from the story.

>> *Go Digital!*
Write your response online. Use your editing checklist.

?

Essential Question

What changes in the environment affect living things?

>> *Go Digital*

What do monarch butterflies do in winter? What do they do in spring? What types of changes affect living things? Write types of changes in the chart.

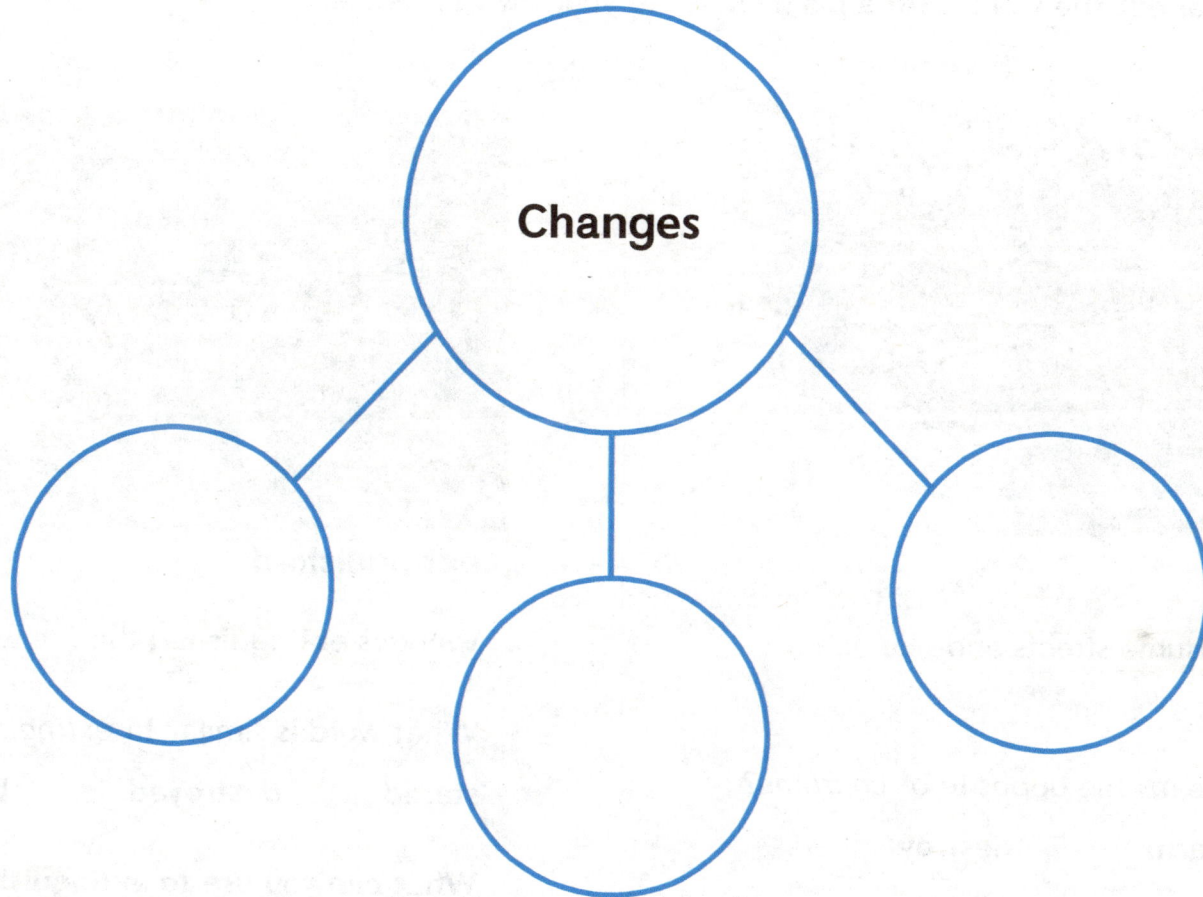

Changes

Discuss how changes in the environment affect living things. Use words from the chart. You can say:

Monarch butterflies fly _____ in the winter.

The types of changes that affect living things are _____.

More Vocabulary

COLLABORATE Look at the picture. Read the word. Then read the sentence. Talk about the word with a partner. Write your own sentence.

consume

Floods can **consume** streets and damage cars.

What word means the opposite of *consume*?

save   farm   destroy

What happens when fires consume trees?

When fires consume trees, it means that

fires _____ trees.

extinguished

Workers **extinguished** the fire with water.

What word is similar to *extinguished*?

stared   destroyed   built

What can you use to extinguish a campfire?

I can use _____ to extinguish a campfire.

Words and Phrases: *already* and *among*

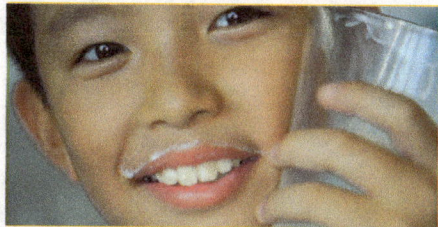

The word *already* means "before now."

Does Chad have any milk?

No, he **already** drank the milk.

The word *among* means "within a group of."

Who is the boy among Ann's friends?

Cal is the boy **among** Ann's friends.

Look at the picture. Read the sentence. Talk with a partner. Write the word that completes each sentence.

I saw a star that is _____

the brightest stars in the sky.

already   among

Grandmother is _____ in the car.

already   among

IZA STOCK/Alamy; Fancy Collection/SuperStock; David Sucsy/E+/Getty Images; m-gucci/iStock/Getty Images Plus

COLLABORATE

1 Talk About It

Look at the photograph. Read the title. Discuss what you see. Use these words.

fire   forest   trees   burning

Write about what you see.

The text is about _____

_____.

Where is the fire burning?

The fire is burning in _____

_____.

What happens during a forest fire?

_____

_____

_____

Take notes as you read the text.

Forests on Fire

Essential Question

? **What changes in the environment affect living things?**

Read about how forest fires effect plants, animals, and people.

A few years ago, red squirrels were rescued from a wildfire that had already destroyed thousands of acres of land. The fire had to be **extinguished** before the squirrels could return to the wild. Forests fires are part of nature, so it is important to understand why they happen.

Fires Destroy and Produce

Like rainstorms, wildfires are a force of nature. However, unlike rainstorms, wildfires almost always destroy things. They **consume** everything in their way, including plants, trees, and animals. Sometimes, they take human lives and destroy homes.

However, naturally occurring wildfires produce necessary changes in the environment. Like rain, wildfires allow new life to grow.

The Good Effects of Wildfires

Humans do not cause a naturally occurring wildfire. Three factors must be present for a wildfire to burn. They are fuel, such as dry grasses; oxygen in the atmosphere; and heat to burn the fuel. A lightning strike usually sparks a naturally occurring wildfire.

Wildfires help to regenerate earth. When plant matter decays, wildfires clear it away, so new plant life can grow.

Evgeny_D/iStock/Getty Images

Text Evidence

1 Sentence Structure A C T

Reread the third sentence. What does the pronoun *they* refer to? Underline the text that tells you. What is important?

It is important _____

_____.

2 Comprehension

Compare and Contrast

Reread the second paragraph. Circle the text that tells how wildfires and rainstorms are alike. Underline text that tells how they are different. Write about it.

_____

_____

3 Specific Vocabulary A C T

The word *produce* means "to cause a result." What do wildfires produce? Circle the text.

Wildfires produce _____

_____

Text Evidence

1 Sentence Structure (A C T)

Reread the first two sentences. What does the pronoun *this* refer to? Underline the text that tells you. What causes soil to be more fertile?

Soil becomes fertile when _____

_____.

2 Specific Vocabulary (A C T)

The word *invasive* means "wanting to control an area." Circle the context clue in the next sentence that tells the meaning of *invasive*.

COLLABORATE

3 Talk About It

Reread the last paragraph. Discuss examples of diversity in the forests. Write about it.

In a forest with diversity, there are

_____

_____.

Open cone

New seedling

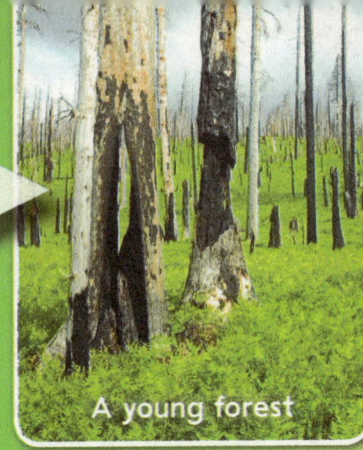
A young forest

The black spruce tree needs heat to open its cones and scatter seeds. Later, a new forest will grow.

Fire also releases nutrients back into the soil. This makes soil more fertile. And fire burns the top leaves of trees, allowing sunlight to reach a forest floor.

Often, the new plant life will have better adaptations to fire than the previous plant. Some species will have fire-resistant roots, leaves, or bark. Others will depend on fire to reproduce.

Stability and Diversity

Stability is among fire's benefits. Fire destroys invasive species. Then the region's own plants can grow, and invasive species does not take over the area.

At the same time, fire encourages diversity. For example, a recently burned forest will have new seedlings. Not far away, in an area struck by fire twenty years earlier, small trees grow. Nearby, in an area with no fires for years, there will be mature trees. This variety in plant life provides food and habitats for different kinds of insects, birds, and mammals. Forests at different stages attract a diversity of animals to the region.

The Effects of Humans

In the past our government misunderstood fires and tried to fight them completely. This policy had a negative impact on the environment. As decayed plant matter built up, it provided more fuel for fires. Consequently, wildfires became fiercer.

Now the government manages wildfires with two strategies. One way is to limit fires before they burn out of control. The other is to set small fires to reduce the amount of fuel in the area.

Unfortunately, fires caused by human carelessness are a problem. Wildfires can have benefits, but fires from human mistakes do not. Fires cannot control themselves, so humans must figure out how best to handle them.

June U.S. Wildfire Activity (2007–2011)

Year	Number of Fires	Acres Burned
2007	9,000	450,000
2008	8,800	650,000
2009	6,500	440,000
2010	4,000	780,000
2011	6,000	1,300,000

Firefighters work to contain small and large forest fires.

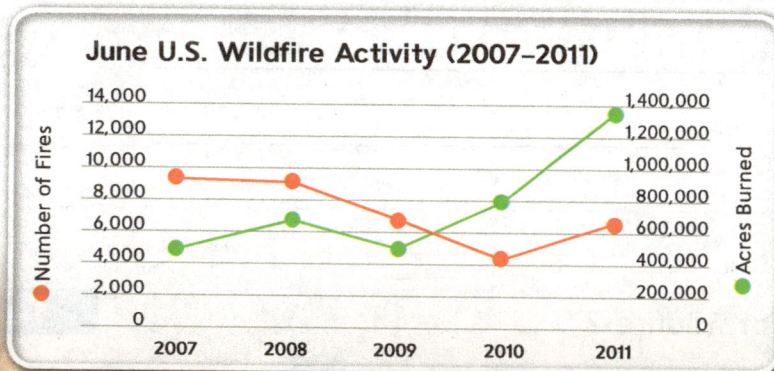

ZUMA Press, Inc./Alamy Stock Photo

Make Connections

? Talk about how wildfires change the environment for plants. **ESSENTIAL QUESTION**

Why is it important for you to be careful around fire? **TEXT TO SELF**

Text Evidence

1 Specific Vocabulary A C T

The word *policy* means "the way of doing something." What was the government policy? Underline the text that tells you.

2 Sentence Structure A C T

Reread the last two sentences of the first paragraph. What happens when decayed plant matter builds up? Circle the two effects.

The two effects are _____

_____

_____

3 Comprehension

Compare and Contrast

Reread the last paragraph. How are wildfires different from fires caused by humans? Put a box around the text that tells you.

One difference is that _____

_____

_____.

35

Respond to the Text

Partner Discussion Work with a partner. Read the questions about "Forest on Fire." Show where you found text evidence. Write the page numbers. Then discuss what you learned.

How do wildfires affect living things?

Wildfires consume and destroy _____

_____.

Wildfires also produce _____

_____.

Text Evidence

Page(s): _____

Page(s): _____

What are the good effects of wildfires?

I read that wildfires help to _____

_____.

Wildfires also provide stability and diversity by _____

_____.

Text Evidence

Page(s): _____

Page(s): _____

Group Discussion Present your answers to the group. Cite text evidence for your ideas. Listen to and discuss the group's opinions.

Write Work with a partner. Look at your notes about "Forests on Fire." Write your answer to the Essential Question. Use text evidence to support your answer. Use vocabulary words in your writing.

> **How do wildfires affect living things?**
>
> Wildfires are dangerous because they destroy_____
>
> _____.
>
> Wildfires are helpful because they produce _____
>
> _____.
>
> People view wildfires as both _____
>
> _____.

Share Writing Present your writing to the class. Discuss their opinions. Talk about their ideas. Explain why you agree or disagree with their ideas. You can say:

I agree with _____.

I do not agree because _____.

Jane

Take Notes About the Text I took notes about the text on the chart to answer the question: *How do wildfires harm and help a forest?*

pages 32–35

Topic	Topic
Wildfires are harmful.	Wildfires are helpful.
Details	**Details**
Wildfires destroy plants and animals. Sometimes wildfires hurt people. Wildfires destroy homes.	Wildfires burn away rotten vegetation. Wildfires make soil more fertile. Wildfires get rid of nonnative plants.

Write About the Text I used notes from my chart to write a paragraph about wildfires.

Student Model: *Informative Text*

Wildfires harm and help a forest. Wildfires destroy forests. They burn plants, animals, humans, and homes. But wildfires can be productive, too. They burn decay. Then new plants can grow. Soil gets fertile. When fires burn the top parts of trees, sunlight reaches the forest floor. New plants sprout. Wildfires damage a forest, but they also help the forest to grow.

TALK ABOUT IT

COLLABORATE

Text Evidence

Draw a box around a sentences that comes from the notes. Does Jane use the information as a detail?

Grammar

Circle an adjective that describes the soil. Why does Jane use this adjective?

Connect Ideas

Underline the sentences that tell about how wildfires destroy. How can you use the word *because* to combine the sentences and connect the ideas?

Your Turn

COLLABORATE

Write about how fires started by humans can help or hurt a forest. Use text evidence in your writing.

>> Go Digital!
Write your response online. Use your editing checklist.

? **Essential Question**

How can scientific knowledge change over time?

>> *Go Digital*

What is the scientist doing? What kinds of things help scientists get new information? How does new information change scientific knowledge? Write words in the chart.

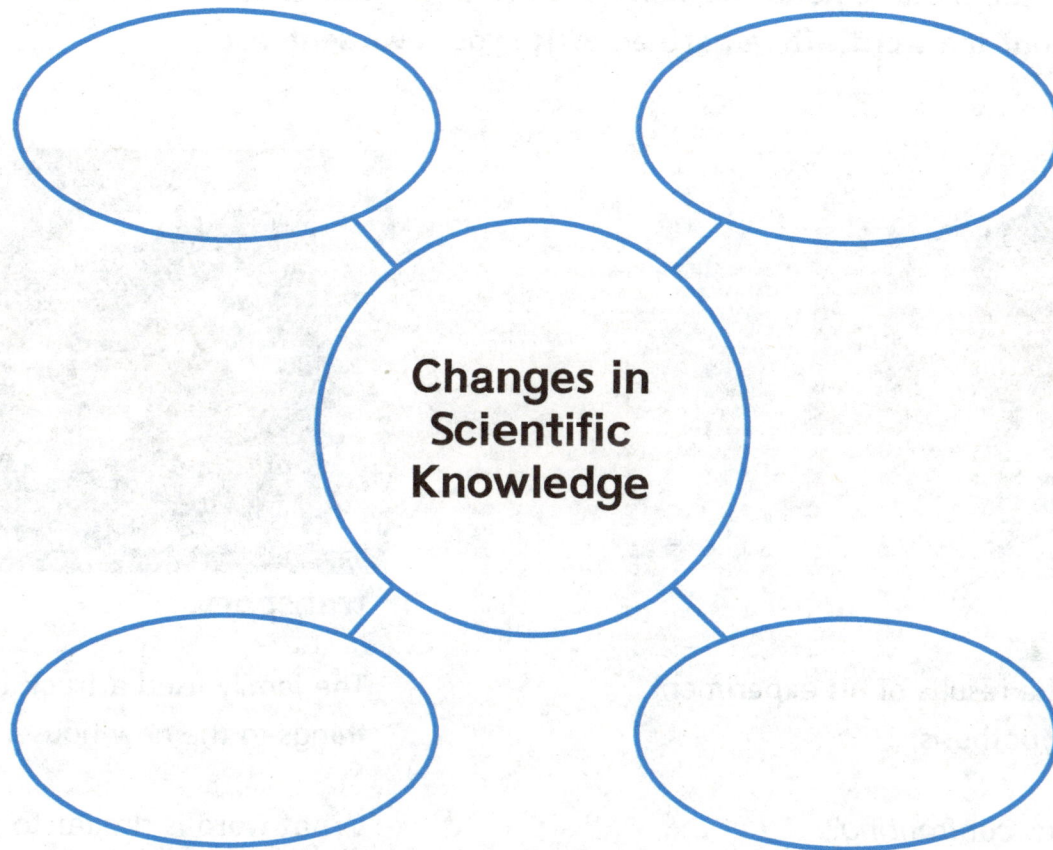

Changes in Scientific Knowledge

Discuss how new information changes scientific knowledge. Use words from the chart. Complete the sentences.

Scientists get new information from _____.

New information changes scientific knowledge when _____

_____.

©Kip Evans/Alamy Stock Photo

More Vocabulary

COLLABORATE Look at the picture. Read the word. Then read the sentence. Talk about the word with a partner. Write your own sentence.

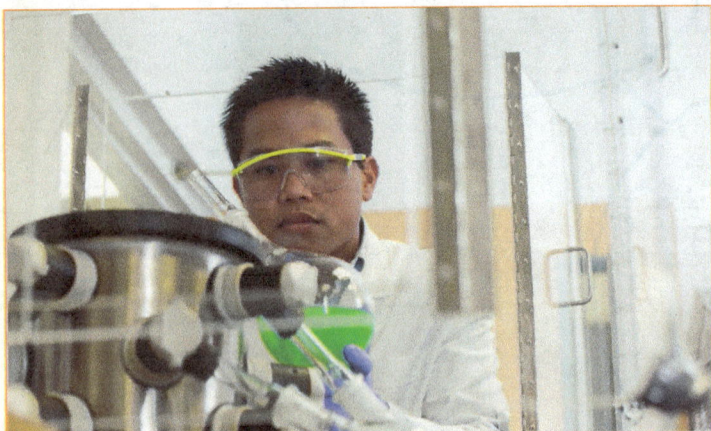

confronting

Mario is testing the results of his experiment to **confront** his hypothesis.

What word means *confronting*?

telling   **facing**   **showing**

What problems do scientists confront by testing the results?

Scientists confront _____

by testing the results.

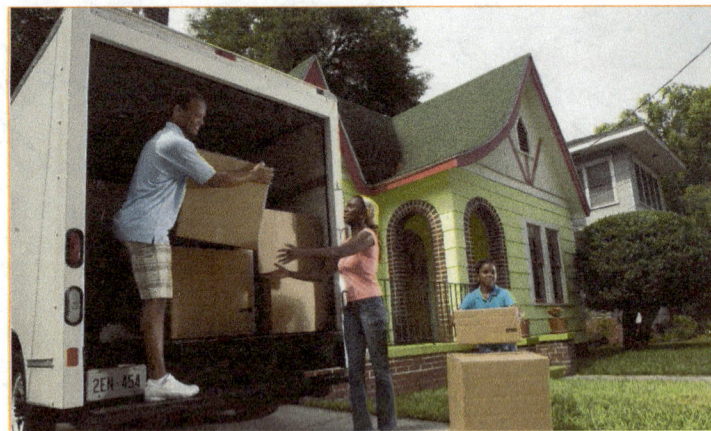

transport

The family used a truck to **transport** their things to the new house.

What word is similar to *transport*?

help   **leave**   **carry**

What do you use to transport your books?

I use _____ to *transport* my books.

42

Words and Phrases: *farther* and *long ago*

The word *farther* means "more distant than before; further."

Are the climbers moving closer to the bottom of the mountain?

No, the climbers are moving **farther** away.

The phrase *long ago* means "a long time before"

Are dinosaurs alive today?

No, *dinosaurs* lived **long ago.**

Look at the picture. Read the sentence. Talk with a partner. Write the word that completes each sentence.

Grandma's house is _____ down the street.

farther   **long ago**

People drove and rode in cars like this _____.

farther   **long ago**

COLLABORATE

1 Talk About It

Look at the photograph. Read the title. Talk about what you see. Use these words.

Earth space planet continents oceans

Write about what you see.

The text is about _____

_____ .

What do you see in the photograph?

I see _____

_____ .

Where was the picture taken?

The picture was taken from _____

_____ .

Take notes as you read the text.

CHANGING VIEWS OF EARTH

NASA-GFSC Image created by Reto Stockli with the help of Alan Nelson, under the leadership of Fritz Hasler

Essential Question

? How can scientific knowledge change over time?

Read about how our understanding of Earth has changed over time.

On the Ground, Looking Around

When you plan an outdoor activity, you probably check the weather forecast. After centuries of scientific developments, we now have the ability to predict storms and droughts. To do this, we looked up at the skies to learn more about life on Earth.

Long ago, people based their knowledge on what they saw and heard. However, they could not understand simple things **confronting** them, such as the Sun. For centuries, people believed that Earth stayed in place and the Sun moved around it. This was the geocentric model.

In the early 1600s, Galileo used a new tool called the telescope to study the night sky. As a result of his heightened vision, he saw the stars, planets, and celestial spheres more clearly. This led Galileo to support a new model of the solar system. A scientist named Copernicus had proposed a heliocentric model. In this model, the Sun did not orbit Earth. Instead, Earth orbited the Sun.

Galileo's telescope helped prove that the heliocentric view was correct. ▶

The left diagram shows the geocentric model.
The right diagram shows the heliocentric model.

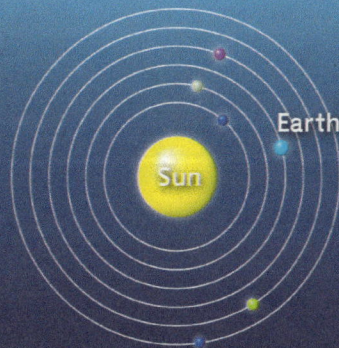

Earth   Sun

Earth

Sun

Hulton Archive/Getty Images

Text Evidence 🔍

1 Sentence Structure Ⓐ Ⓒ Ⓣ

Reread the last sentence in the second paragraph. Underline who went up to the sky. What does the pronoun *themselves* tell you?

The pronoun themselves tells me

about _____.

2 Comprehension
Cause and Effect

Reread the last paragraph. What caused scientists to use aircraft to observe weather? Box the text.

Scientists used aircraft because

_____

_____.

COLLABORATE

3 Talk About It

Compare technology in 1700s and early 1900s. Support your answer with text evidence. Write about it.

One difference is _____

_____

_____.

In the Sky, Looking Down

New technology gave scientists better ways to study theories. Instruments such as the thermometer and barometer helped them study weather patterns. However, they wanted to study the sky, where weather actually happens.

In the mid-1700s, scientists did just that! They used hot-air balloons to **transport** tools into the sky. Sometimes scientists themselves went up to the sky in balloons!

However, scientists were studying only the lower layers of Earth's atmosphere. They wanted to go higher.

In the early 1900s, aircraft provided a safer way to observe weather. Kites and balloons could rise up to three kilometers. But airplanes could give information from five kilometers or higher. Yet scientists dreamed of reaching ever higher.

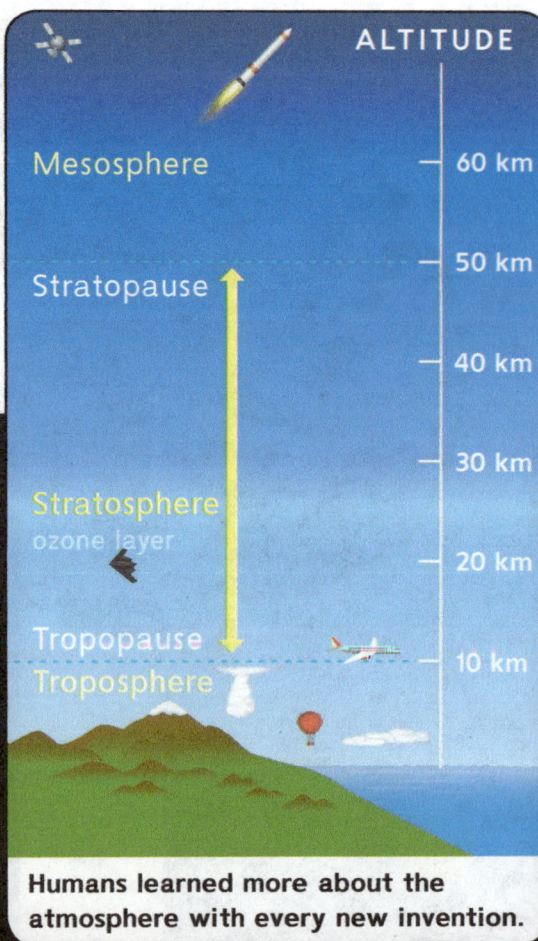

ALTITUDE

Mesosphere — 60 km

Stratopause — 50 km

— 40 km

— 30 km

Stratosphere
ozone layer — 20 km

Tropopause — 10 km
Troposphere

Humans learned more about the atmosphere with every new invention.

Out in Space, Looking Back Home

Today powerful rockets are used to put satellites in orbit around Earth. Scientists can study the composition and thinness of the layers in the atmosphere. Thanks to all the scientific knowledge, weather predictions are much more reliable.

NASA sent satellites to collect data about planets and galaxies. They provide accurate data that scientists can analyze. As a result, scientists can develop more reliable models about Earth's systems.

Today, space missions venture farther and farther from home. Even so, nothing compares to seeing Earth the old way, with our eyes. Views of Earth from space fascinate nearly everyone. Astronaut Joseph Allen talked about going to the Moon. He said, "No one suggested that we should do it to look at the Earth. But that may in fact be the most important reason."

Brand X Pictures/PunchStock

Satellites only last for a limited number of years in space. Then they must be replaced.

Make Connections

?

How did technology affect our knowledge of Earth?
ESSENTIAL QUESTION

How has your knowledge of Earth changed over time?
TEXT TO SELF

Text Evidence

1 Specific Vocabulary Ⓐ Ⓒ Ⓣ

The word *reliable* means "trusted." Why can scientists make reliable predictions? Circle the text.

Scientists can make reliable predictions because _____

_____.

2 Sentence Structure Ⓐ Ⓒ Ⓣ

Reread Joseph Allen's words in the last paragraph. What does the pronoun *it* refer to? Underline the text in the previous sentence.

COLLABORATE

3 Talk About It

Reread the last paragraph. Discuss what Joseph Allen thought was the most important reason for going to the Moon. Support your answer with text evidence. Write about it.

Allen thought the most important reason was _____

_____.

47

Respond to the Text

COLLABORATE **Partner Discussion** Work with a partner. Read the questions about "Changing Views of Earth." Show where you found text evidence. Write the page numbers. Then discuss what you learned.

What did people believe about Earth in the past?

I read that long ago people thought the Sun moved around _____

_____.

Then Galileo helped prove Copernicus's idea that Earth moves around

_____.

Text Evidence 🔍

Page(s): _____

Page(s): _____

How has technology helped scientists make new discoveries?

In the 1700s, scientists used kites and _____.

In the early 1900s, scientists used _____.

Now, scientists use rockets and _____.

Text Evidence 🔍

Page(s): _____

Page(s): _____

Page(s): _____

COLLABORATE **Group Discussion** Present your answers to the group. Cite text evidence for your ideas. Listen to and discuss the group's opinions.

Write Work with a partner. Look at your notes about "Changing Views of Earth." Write your answer to the Essential Question. Use text evidence to support your answer. Use vocabulary words in your writing.

COLLABORATE

How has knowledge about Earth changed over time?

Long ago, people thought that _____.

To learn more about Earth, scientists used _____

_____.

Examples of things scientists used are _____.

Today, scientists use _____

_____.

The new technology helps scientists _____.

Share Writing Present your writing to the class. Discuss their opinions. Talk about their ideas. Explain why you agree or disagree with their ideas. You can say:

I agree with _____.

I do not agree because _____.

Leland Bobbe/Photodisc/Getty Images

April

Take Notes About the Text I took notes on the chart to answer the question: *How have people changed the way they make weather predictions over time?*

pages 44–47

First

Long ago, people used what they heard and saw to predict the weather.

Next

In the 1700s, scientists used kites and hot air balloons.

Then

In the 1900s, scientists used airplanes to study weather.

Last

Today, scientists use satellites to study weather.

Write About the Text I used notes from my chart to write an informative text about predicting weather.

Student Model: *Informative Text*

Long ago, people used what they saw to predict the weather. They also used what they heard to predict weather. Next, in the mid-1700s, scientists used kites and balloons to study weather in the sky. Then, during the 1900s, they used airplanes to study weather higher in the atmosphere. Today, scientists use satellites to study weather from space. It is more reliable to predict weather now.

COLLABORATE

TALK ABOUT IT

Text Evidence
Circle a sentence that comes from the notes. Why does April use this information?

Grammar
Underline an adjective in the last sentence. What does the adjective describe?

Condense Ideas
Draw a box around the first two sentences. How can you condense the ideas to write one sentence?

COLLABORATE

Your Turn
Why did the author use Joseph Allen's quote? Use text evidence in your writing.

>> Go Digital!
Write your response online. Use your editing checklist.

Essential Question
How do natural events and human activities affect the environment?

>> *Go Digital*

What is the man's job? How do bees help him? How does he help the bees? What natural and human activities affect the environment? Write words in the chart.

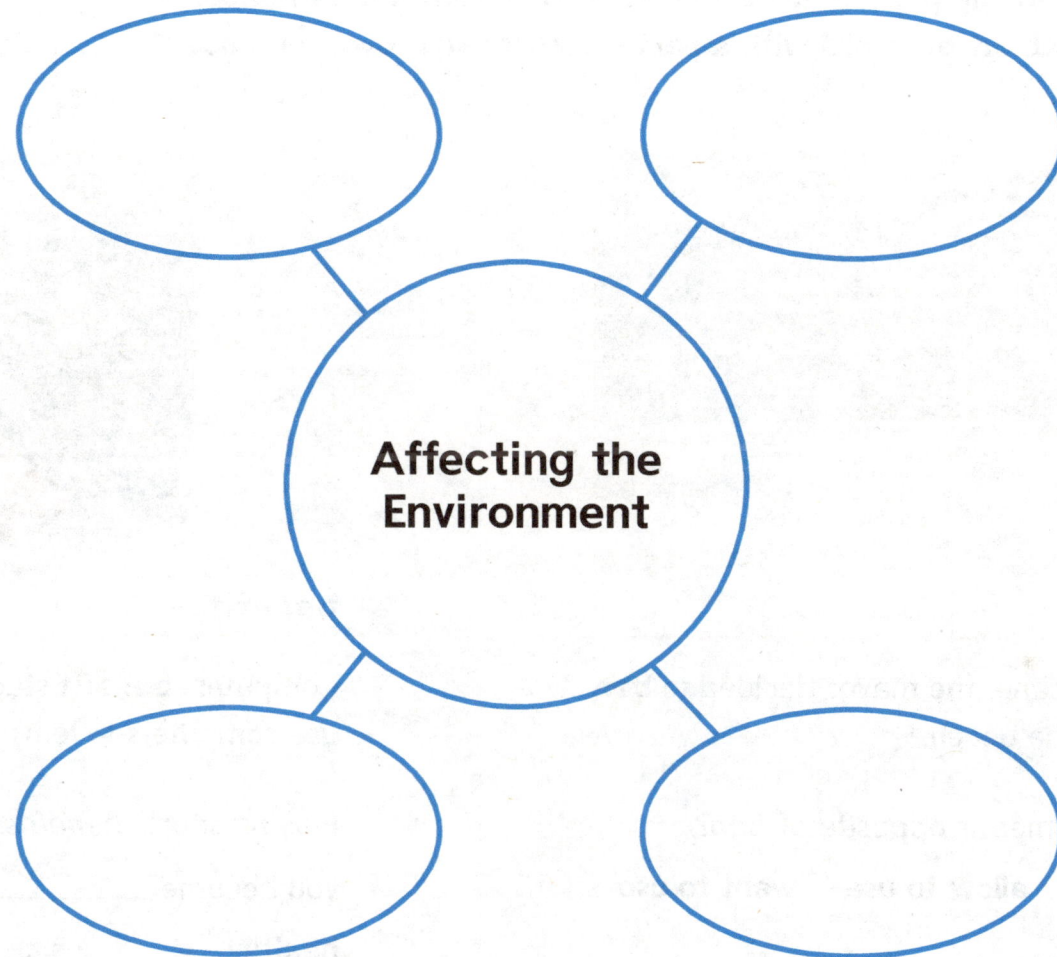

Affecting the Environment

Discuss how natural and human activities affect the environment. Use words from the chart. You can say:

The man helps bees by _____. The bees help the man by _____

_____. One activity that affects the environment is _____.

More Vocabulary

Look at the picture. Read the word. Then read the sentence. Talk about the word with a partner. Write your own sentence.

ban

After the hurricane, the mayor decided to **ban** swimming at the beach.

Which phrase means opposite of *ban*?

refuse to use   allow to use   want to use

What would you like to ban at school?

I would like to ban _____ at school.

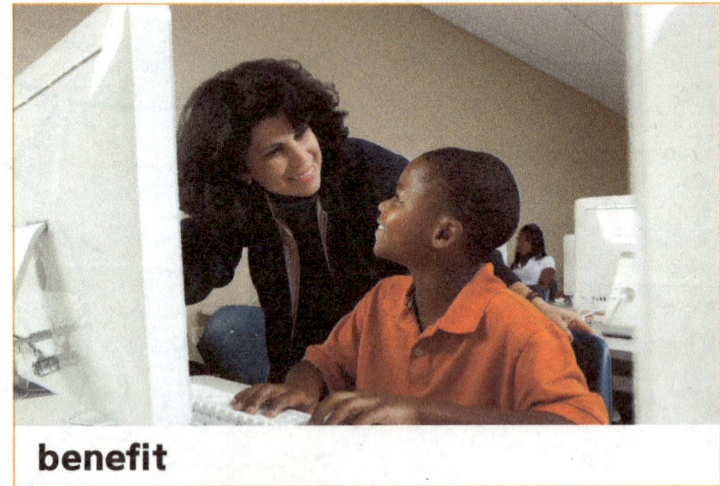

benefit

Computers **benefit** students because students use computers to learn.

Playing sports *benefits* you because

you become _____.

healthy   sick   excited

How does sleeping 8 hours a day benefit you at school?

Sleeping 8 hours a day helps me at school

because _____.

Words and Phrases: *side effects* and *worse off*

The phrase *side effects* means "unplanned or unexpected results."

What is one positive side effect of using computers?

One positive **side effect** is that people can communicate from far away places.

The phrase *worse off* means "in a less fortunate condition."

Why are people worse off without electricity?

People are **worse off** because lights and machines do not work.

COLLABORATE Look at the picture. Read the sentence. Talk with a partner. Write the word that completes each sentence.

One _____ of the Internet is that few people write letters.

       side effect   **worse off**

Many people will be _____ after the store closes.

       side effect   **worse off**

COLLABORATE

1 Talk About It

Look at the photograph. Read the title. Talk about what you see. Use these words.

animals   oranges   leaves   plants

Write about what you see.

This text is about _____

_____

_____.

What do you see in the picture?

I see _____

_____.

Where do oranges grow?

Oranges grow _____

_____.

Take notes as you read the text.

Essential Question

? **How do natural events and human activities affect the environment?**

Read different views on the arrival of new species into our country.

Oranges and chickens are examples of nonnative species.

Kirk Weddle/Photodisc/Getty Images

Should Plants and Animals from Other Places Live Here?

New Arrivals Welcome

Nonnative species are good for business. They taste good, too!

Some of America's most important imports are plants and animals that come from other regions or countries. They are called *nonnative species*. Nonnative species are *invasive* when they harm the environment, our health, or the economy. Invasive species can take over an area and cause native wildlife to decline. Yet we would be a lot worse off without some of them.

For example, in Florida about 2,000 species of familiar plants and animals are nonnative. Oranges, chickens, and sugarcane are nonnative. In fact, about 90 percent of farm sales are nonnative species.

Some scientists bring in nonnative species to help control insects and pests that harm crops. For example, scientists brought Vedalia beetles from Australia to eat insects that killed citrus fruit. The Vedalia beetles completed their mission without any side effects. They **benefit** citrus farmers.

Many dogs and cats we love come from other countries. Would you want to **ban** Labrador retrievers or Siamese cats? Creatures like these make our lives and our nation better!

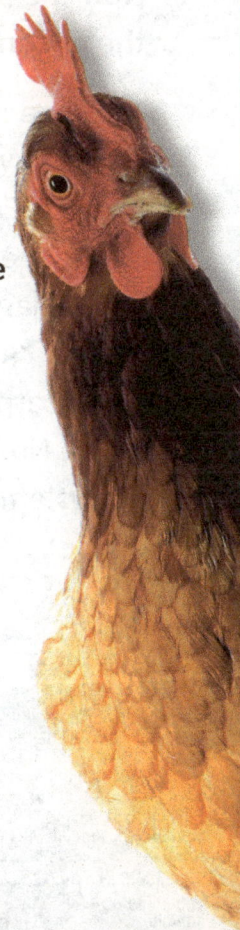

Text Evidence

1 Specific Vocabulary A C T

The meaning of *imports* appears in the sentence. Underline a context clue that tells about the meaning. Circle a synonym of *imports* in the next sentence.

2 Sentence Structure A C T

Reread the third sentence. How do nonnative species become invasive? Underline the text that tells you.

Nonnative species become invasive

by _____

_____.

3 Comprehension
Author's Point of View

Reread the second paragraph. What evidence does the author use to tell about the author's point of view? Underline the evidence.

The author uses as evidence _____

_____

_____.

Text Evidence

1 Sentence Structure A C T

Reread the third sentence. Circle the text that the pronoun *they* refers to. Underline the text that the pronoun *there* refers to.

Pythons are in the Everglades

because _____

_____.

2 Comprehension
Author's Point of View

Reread the second paragraph. What evidence does the author use to tell the point of view? Put a box around the evidence.

COLLABORATE

3 Talk About It

Discuss whether you agree or disagree with the author's point of view. Support your answer with text evidence. Write about it.

_____

_____

COUNTERPOINT POINT

A Growing Problem

Thousands of foreign species threaten our country.

Visitors to the Florida Everglades expect to see alligators. However, over 150,000 pythons from Southeast Asia live there. They probably ended up there because pet owners dumped them there. Now the pythons are a threat to the endangered native species.

Some nonnative species are harmful when they become invasive. Each year the United States spends $137 billion to repair damage nonnative species cause. For example, the Asian carp invaded the Great Lakes. Now, it threatens the ecosystem. Asian carp have big appetites, so the population of native fish has declined.

Some germs are also invasive species. They are very harmful to humans. One germ, the avian influenza virus, came to the United States carried by birds. This microbe can cause a serious lung disorder.

Sometimes people introduce a nonnative species to improve the environment. However, this creates unexpected problems. A hundred years ago, melaleuca trees came from Australia to Florida to stabilize swampy areas. Now millions of trees crowd out native species.

The facts about alien invasion lead to one conclusion: We must remove invasive species and stop new ones from entering.

Irina Mos/Shutterstock.com

Nonnative Species: Benefits and Costs

About 50,000 nonnative species live in the United States. These four examples show the positive and negative impacts they can have.

SPECIES	NATIVE LAND	WHEN AND HOW INTRODUCED TO U.S.	POSITIVE IMPACT	NEGATIVE IMPACT
Horse	Europe	Early 1500s, on purpose	Used for work, transportation, and recreation	Made large wars possible
Kudzu	Asia	Early 1800s, on purpose	Stops soil erosion	Crowds out native plants
Olives	Middle East and Europe	Early 1700s, on purpose, cultivation began in 1800s	Major food and cooking oil source, important industry in California	Most olives must be imported because they do not grow everywhere.
Mediterranean Fruit Fly	Sub-Saharan Africa	1929 (first recorded), accidentally	May be a food source for creatures such as spiders	Destroys 400 species of plants, including citrus and vegetable crops

The melaleuca plant has taken over this marsh.

Make Connections

? Talk about the uses and harmful effects of nonnative species in the United States.

ESSENTIAL QUESTION

Would you give up eating chicken because it is nonnative? Explain your reasons.

TEXT TO SELF

(t to b) Ingram Publishing; Matt Meadows/Photolibrary/Getty Images; Emilio Simion/Photodisc/Getty Images; Jack Dykinga/USDA

Text Evidence

1 Specific Vocabulary (A)(C)(T)

The word *impacts* means "effects," and it is used as a noun in the sentence. What are the different types of impact? Circle the text. What does the word *impact* refer to? Underline the text.

2 Comprehension
Author's Point of View

Reread the chart. Which nonnative species were introduced unintentionally to the United States? Circle the species.

COLLABORATE

3 Talk About It

Choose one nonnative species and discuss whether it is invasive or not. Support your answer with text evidence. Then write about it.

_____

_____

_____

Respond to the Text

Partner Discussion Work with a partner. Read the questions about "Should Plants and Animals from Other Places Live Here?" Show where you found text evidence. Write the page numbers. Then discuss what you learned.

COLLABORATE

How do nonnative species help us?

I read that in Florida plants and animals come from _____.

Vadalia beetles help control _____.

Our pets come from _____.

Text Evidence 🔍

Page(s): _____

Page(s): _____

Page(s): _____

How do nonnative species cause harm?

Nonnative species can destroy _____.

Nonnative species become invasive by _____

_____.

An example of invasive species is _____.

Text Evidence 🔍

Page(s): _____

Page(s): _____

Page(s): _____

Group Discussion Present your answers to the group. Cite text evidence for your ideas. Listen to and discuss the group's opinions.

COLLABORATE

Write Work with a partner. Look at your notes about "Should Plants and Animals from Other Places Live Here?" Write your answer to the Essential Question. Use text evidence to support your answer. Use vocabulary words in your writing.

How do nonnative species affect the environment?

People bring nonnative species into the country to _____

_____.

Invasive species, such as Asian carp, harm _____

_____.

Nonnative species affect our environment because _____

_____.

Share Writing Present your writing to the class. Discuss their opinions. Talk about their ideas. Explain why you agree or disagree with their ideas. You can say:

I agree with _____.

I do not agree because _____.

Write to Sources

Vince

Take Notes About the Text I took notes about the text on the idea web to answer the question: *Should nonnative species enter the United States? Write about your opinion.*

pages 56–59

Evidence
Scientists brought Vedalia beetles to eat insects that eat citrus fruit.

Evidence
Beetles ate insects harming the fruit. Did not need pesticides.

Opinion
Nonnative species should enter the United States.

Evidence
Florida has many nonnative species that are familiar to us.

Evidence
Many pets are nonnative species.

Write About the Text I used notes from my idea web to write an opinion.

Student Model: *Argument*

I think nonnative species should enter the United States. For example, scientists brought Vedalia beetles. The beetles ate the pests that were killing citrus fruit. Farmers did not have to use pesticides. Many plants and animals in Florida are nonnative species. Examples are oranges and chickens. Also, many pets are nonnative species, too.

TALK ABOUT IT

COLLABORATE

Text Evidence
Draw a box around a sentence that comes from the notes. Does the information support Vince's opinion?

Grammar
Underline past-tense and present-tense verbs. When does Vince use past-tense verbs?

Connect Ideas
Circle the sentences about Vedalia beetles. How can you combine the sentences into one sentence?

Your Turn
COLLABORATE

Should pythons be allowed in the United States? Write about your opinion. Use text evidence in your writing.

>> Go Digital
Write your response online. Use your editing checklist.